Michael B...

MARXISM, FREEDOM AND THE STATE

Translated and Edited with
a Biographical Sketch by

K. J. KENAFICK

FREEDOM PRESS
LONDON 1998

First published 1950
by Freedom Press
84b Whitechapel High Street
London E1 7QX

Reprinted 1984, 1990, 1998

Printed in Great Britain
by Aldgate Press, London E1

Contents

*Liberty for all, and a natural
respect for that liberty: such
are the essential conditions of
international solidarity.*
BAKUNIN.

TO THE MEMORY
OF
J. W. (Chummy) FLEMING
(1864–1950)
WHO, FOR NEARLY SIXTY YEARS
UPHELD THE CAUSE OF FREEDOM
AT THE
YARRA BANK OPEN AIR FORUM
MELBOURNE, AUSTRALIA

Foreword

IN MY BOOK *Michael Bakunin and Karl Marx,* I stated in a footnote that I intended to reprint certain passages from Bakunin in a booklet to be entitled *Marxism, Anarchism and the State.* The present work is a fulfilment of that intention; but I have slightly altered the title, because on reflection, I felt that Bakunin was here treating of wider and deeper matters than merely the merits of one political philosophy as against another. He was treating of the whole question of man's freedom in relation to society, to the community.

This question is the supreme question of our generation. On its solution depends the fate of the human race; for if the answer to the question of man's freedom in relation to the community is to be the totalitarian answer that he has none, then indeed can the march of human progress be said to have come to its end. And that end, bearing in mind the circumstances of this atomic age can only be amidst war and universal destruction.

In many parts of his writings, Bakunin has given his views on the nature and possibilities of human freedom—which he sharply differentiated from egoism and self centred individualism. Apart from that reproduced on the first page of the extracts, perhaps the best definition he has given is that couched in the following words:

"We understand by liberty, on the one hand, the development, as complete as possible of all the natural faculties of each individual, and, on the other hand, his independence, not as regards natural and social laws but as regards all the laws imposed by other human wills, whether collective or separate.

"When we demand the liberty of the masses, we do not in the least claim to abolish any of the natural influences of any individual or of any group of individuals which exercise their action on them. What we want is the abolition of artificial, privileged, legal, official, influences." (*Michael Bakunin and Karl Marx,* p. 300.)

With this view of liberty is linked Bakunin's view of authority, which he by no means equates with organisation and self-discipline, things which, in themselves, he regarded as very desirable. What he meant by "authority", namely the *right* to command or to enforce obedience, was considered by him to be fundamentally of religious origin. The idea of an authoritarianism that it is our *duty* to obey authority, is derived, according to his theory from religious origins, even when it has later taken political forms. Hence the opposition to religion, which takes a prominent position in his writings, much more so than in those of the Marxians, and which sometimes is rather violently expressed.

There is also another reason for the criticism of religion and churches that is to be found so frequently in his writings, and that is the close connection between religion and the State which distinguishes the Hegelian philosophy against which Bakunin had rebelled. It is pointed out by Gide and Rist: "The State, according to Hegel, is an aggression of the spirit realising itself in the conscience of the world, while nature is an expression of the same spirit without the conscience, an *alter ego*—a spirit in bondage. God moving in the world has made the State possible. Its foundation is in the might of reason realising itself in will. It is necessary to think of it not merely as a given State or a particular institution, but of its essence or idea as a real manifestation of God. Every State, of whatever kind it may be, partakes of this divine essence." (*A History of Economic Doctrines*, p. 435.)

Now this close identification of the spirit of God and the spirit of the State is reason enough why Bakunin, as an enemy of the State, should also have considered it necessary to attack religion. Thus, the term "God and the State" later applied by its editors to a fragment of his works, is quite fitting. The Marxians, on the other hand, as adherents of the State, and as champions of authority, found no such necessity for making a frontal attack on religion, and encountered accordingly much less of the animous of religiously-minded people than was the fate of the Anarchists.

Opinions may differ in the Socialist movement itself as to the relative importance to be given to the discussion of the religious questions; but the matter is mentioned here only in order to explain Bakunin's attitude and to show that it had a logical development, whether or not it were the best tactic to pursue, and whether or not its fundamental assumptions were correct.

As will be indicated in more detail in the following biography, the extracts printed in this volume are taken mainly from those writings of Bakunin touching on his controversy with Marx and therefore belong to the years 1870-72; but the passages dealing with the nature and characteristics of the State in general are mostly taken from *Federalism, Socialism and Anti-Theologianism* written in 1867, and based, as the title indicates, on the above-mentioned close connection, to his mind, between the State and religion.

It is not only the question of the relation of Marxian doctrines to those of freedom and of the State, so much discussed in the following pages that gives them interest and importance, but also the light they throw on the system that now exists in Soviet Russia, and which calls itself "Socialist" and "democratic", where it is, in reality, neither the one nor the other, but essentially capitalistic and totalitarian or, as Bakunin expressed it in a passage to be quoted later "all work performed in the employ of the State". Bakunin showed in the early seventies of the nineteenth century that such a system *must* result if it is attempted to transform society on an authoritarian basis; the existence in the middle of the twentieth century of that portentious phenomenon, the Soviet Government, has proved him up to the hilt to be right. In the words of his friend and collaborator, James Guillaume, "How could one want an equalitarian and free society to issue from an authoritarian organisation? It is impossible."

Melbourne, 1950.   K. J. KENAFICK.

Life of Bakunin

MICHAEL ALEXANDROVITCH BAKUNIN was born on 30th May, 1814, in the Russian province of Tvar. He was the eldest son of a retired diplomat, who was a member of the ancient Russian nobility. Young Michael passed his boyhood on the family estate, and gained there an insight into the peasant mentality which is reflected in his later writings.

At the age of fifteen, after a good home education under tutors, he was sent to St. Petersburg to study for and enter the Artillery School. After five years of military studies, he was posted as ensign to a regiment stationed in Poland; but the monotonous life of a remote garrison soon proved highly unpalatable to this very sociable and high-spirited young aristocrat. He threw up his commission and the whole military career and adopted instead that of a student in Moscow.

The adolescence and young manhood of Bakunin were spent under the iron despotism of the Tsar Nicholas I, the most consistently reactionary that Russia had ever known and the most rigidly repressive till the dictatorship of Joseph Stalin. Under this regime every type of liberalism of even the mildest kind, whether in politics, literature, or religion, was ruthlessly crushed. In philosophy alone did there seem to be any chance for discussion, and those who would in Western countries have turned to politics devoted their attention in Russia to philosophy. Bakunin was one of these and in fact at this time his interest in politics appears to have been nil. His favourite philosophers were Fichte and Hegel; from the former he learned that freedom, liberty, independence were the highest expression of the moral law; from the latter, the dominating philosopher of the time, he gained a knowledge of the Dialectic, the theory that all life and history constitute a process of the reconciliation of opposites on a higher plane—

or, as Hegel expressed it, thesis, antithesis and synthesis. From this there naturally arose a theory of historic evolution.

Five years of Bakunin's life (1835-40) were spent in the study of philosophy at Moscow, and then he went to Berlin to imbibe more knowledge of his subject at its fountainhead. The political and intellectual atmosphere of Germany, though reactionary compared to those of France and England, was almost progressive as compared with Russia and some of the younger adherents of Hegel began to develop Radical ideas from his doctrine of the Dialectic. Prominent among these was Ludwig Feuerbach, whose book *The Essence of Christianity* took a decidedly materialistic, in fact, atheistic attitude. It converted many young intellectuals to its viewpoint and among these were Karl Marx, Friedrich Engels and Michael Bakunin. The latter's intellectual evolution had now begun—the evolution that was to turn him from an orthodox subject of the Tsar into a Materialist, a Revolutionary Socialist, and an Anarchist.

In 1842 he went to Dresden in Saxony and in October published in Arnold Ruge's *Deutsche Jahrbuecher* an article entitled "Reaction in Germany" which led to revolutionary conclusions and which ended with words that became celebrated: "Let us put our trust in the eternal spirit which destroys and annihilates only because it is the unsearchable and eternally creative source of all life. The desire for destruction is also a creative desire."

Leaving Saxony which had become too hot to hold him as a result of this article, Bakunin went in 1843 to Switzerland. Here he made the acquaintance of Wilhelm Weitling and his writings. This man was a self-educated German Communist, who preached revolution and Socialism in phrases foreshadowing the later Anarchism. He said for instance: "The perfect society has no government but only an administration, no laws but only obligations, no punishments but means of correction." These sentiments greatly impressed and influenced the liberty-loving Bakunin. But they caused the gaoling of Weitling and when the Tsarist Government heard of Bakunin's connection with him, the young man was summoned back to Russia. He refused to go and was outlawed. He went for a brief period to Brussels and then, early in 1844, to Paris.

Bakunin's sojourn in Paris was of vital importance in his intellectual development. He encountered here two men whose influence on his thought was very great. These men were Karl Marx and Pierre-Joseph Proudhon. Bakunin had many discussions with Marx at this period, and though greatly impressed by the German thinker's real genius, scholarship, and revolutionary zeal and energy, was repelled by his arrogance, egotism, and jealousy. These faults were ones of which Bakunin himself was entirely free, and this temperamental difference alone would have made it difficult for these two great men to get along together, even if their opinions had not been dissimilar in many respects, and if outside influences had not deliberately poisoned their relationships at a later time.

But at this period of the early eighteen forties their differences had not yet matured and Bakunin no doubt learned a good deal from Marx of the doctrine of Historical Materialism which is so important an element in both these great Socialistic thinkers' work.

From Proudhon he learned at this period even more than from Marx. The former can be considered as the father of modern Anarchism, for he utterly rejected the very concept of Authority, in both politics and religion. In his economic views, he advocated a scheme called Mutualism, in which the most important rôle was played by a national bank, based on the mutual confidence of all those who were engaged in production. Bakunin did not take up this idea for he was impressed rather by the Marxian economies and advocated a system of Collectivism, but he thoroughly appreciated the spirit of liberty that breathed through all Proudhon's writings and talk, and he placed him in that respect above Marx, of whom he truly said that the spirit of liberty was lacking in him; he remained from head to foot an Authoritarian.

Towards the end of 1847, Bakunin was expelled from Paris for having delivered a speech advocating freedom for Poland which was so displeasing to the Tsarist Government that it put pressure on the French Government to take action against him. He spent a few months in Brussels, but the revolution of February, 1848, which overthrew King Louis Philippe and established the Second Republic allowed Bakunin to return to Paris and he took a prominent part in the political demonstrations of the day. But he was soon attracted by the rising revolutionary movements in Central Europe. In Prague he participated in a brief insurrection, and in May, 1849, in another in Dresden. This resulted in his arrest, and finally his extradition to

Russia, which claimed him as a fugitive. He passed eight horrible years in solitary confinement and it was only the death of the implacable Nicholas I and the accession of the milder Alexander II that enabled his family to secure his release. He spent four more years under surveillance in Siberia, where he married. Finally, in 1861, he escaped on an American vessel going to Japan and at the end of the year reached London.

In London he worked for a time with Alexander Herzen, the Russian Liberal, in his publications addressed to the Russian people, went for a while to try to help a Polish insurrection from there, and then settled down in Italy. Here he encountered the religiously-minded Nationalism of Mazzini, a man whom he greatly respected personally (having met him in London), but whose ideas he heartily disliked. This led him to accentuate the anti-patriotic and anti-religious elements in his own ideas, which by this period of the middle eighteen-sixties had become practically those later called "Anarchism".

In 1867 he went to Geneva to attend the inaugural Congress of the League for Peace and Freedom, a bourgeois body of which he thought some use could be made for the purpose of Socialist propaganda. He soon found that this could not be done (his ideas as set out in an article entitled "Federalism, Socialism and Anti-theologism", were far too radical), and instead he concentrated on the First International, which had been founded, largely through the instrumentality of Marx, in 1864. On leaving the League for Peace and Freedom, Bakunin and his friends had formed the Alliance of Socialist Democracy and this body now applied to join the International. The application aroused the suspicions of Marx who felt a jealous possessiveness as regards the International and had a German-minded antipathy to anything coming from a Russian. The initial proposal was therefore turned down and the Alliance was only admitted in sections, and when as a separate body it had been disbanded. (July, 1869.)

In September of the same year, a Congress of the International was held at Basel. This Congress showed itself favourable to Bakunin's view that inheritance should be abolished and rejected Marx's views on this subject. This was the beginning of a breach between Marx and his followers on the one hand and Bakunin and his followers on the other. It was fundamentally a difference on

11

the question as to the rôle of the State in the Socialist programme. The Marxian view was essentially that the State must be used to bring about and consolidate Socialism; the views of the Bakuninists (at this period beginning to be called "Anarchists") was that the State must be abolished, and that it could never under any circumstances be used to attain either Socialism or any form of social justice for the workers.

These differences spread rapidly throughout the International and were deepened and exacerbated in Switzerland (where Bakunin was now settled) by a Russian emigré named Utin, who by methods of character-assassination poisoned Marx's already jealous and vindictive mind still further against Bakunin. The latter rightly resented the campaign of calumny which was now launched against him but he was of a tolerant and generous disposition and for all his resentment against Marx's tactics (only too prophetic of later "Communist" methods) never failed to acknowledge Marx's greatness as Socialist and thinker. He even began at this time a Russian translation of *Marx's Capital*, a book he highly admired, and whose economic doctrines he enthusiastically supported.

In the early part of 1870, Bakunin was mainly occupied in trying to stir up the Russian people to insurrection. This activity was in collaboration with a fanatical young revolutionary named Sergei Nechayev. The latter had committed a political murder in Russia and deceived Bakunin into condoning this act. He also published a "Revolutionary Catechism" which has often been mistaken for a production of Bakunin's, and which preaches the most violent and amoral tactics against existing society. Internal evidence shows that it cannot be Bakunin's for he was not an advocate of such opinions; and when he finally became aware of Nechayev's unscrupulousness he broke with him. The fugitive was later extradited to Russia and died in jail. The whole episode did Bakunin considerable harm, giving him because of his association with Nechayev, a reputation for violence and amoralism which was quite undeserved.

The Franco-German war which broke out in July, 1870, led to the writing of Bakunin's most important works. He looked to Social Revolution on the part of peasants and workers both to overthrow the reactionary regime of Napoleon III and to repel the German invaders under the direction of Bismarck. With the purpose of stirring up such a movement he wrote *A Letter to a Frenchman,* and then in September after the fall of the Second Empire and the establishment of the Third Republic, went to Lyons to launch an Anarchist rising. Through lack of determination and support by the workers' leaders themselves, despite Bakunin's demand for energetic action, the movement failed after an initial and brief success, and he fled to Marseilles, and thence back to Locarno, whence he had come to Lyons.

This fiasco deeply embittered and depressed Bakunin. He had lost all faith in the bourgeoisie since their turning on the workers in the revolutions of 1848; but now even the workers had shown themselves supine, and he became very pessimistic about their future. Arising out of these events he now wrote his greatest work, *The Knouto-Germanic Empire and the Social Revolution.* The title implied an alliance betwen the knout of the Russian Tsar and the new German Empire of Bismarck and Wilhelm I to crush the social revolution. It became a very voluminous work, treating in an extremely discursive way all manner of subjects, political, historical, economic, religious, philosophical, metaphysical, ethical and even astronomical, for as an Appendix to it Bakunin gave an exposition of the ideas of the System of Nature which he held and which was a complete and consistent Materialism. The piece known as "God and the State" is merely a fragment of this greater work, which is indeed Bakunin's "Magnum opus", his testament, as he called it. He worked at it intermittently from the close of 1870 to the close of 1872 and even then never succeeded in finishing it.*

The Paris Commune of March-May, 1871, interested him greatly though he no longer had any illusions about a workers' victory in any near future. He considered however that the events of the Commune gave a practical justification of his theories as against those of the Marxians, and a study of that historic episode would seem to justify his contention. In this same year, 1871, he had a controversy with Mazzini who had attacked both the International and the Commune, the former as being anti-nationalist and the latter as being atheistic and therefore both being abhorrent to Mazzini's religious nationalism. Bakunin respectfully but trenchantly replied in a pamphlet called *The*

---

* Sections of this work, written in November and December, 1872, have been quoted at length in the text.

Political Theology of Mazzini which had a wide circulation in Italy and a great effect on the Italian working class, which largely became imbued with Anarchist ideas. In Spain also, Bakunin's ideas bore fruit and to a lesser extent in France.

In 1872 he was occupied with the coming Congress of the International at the Hague. This meeting, which was held in September, was "packed" by the Marxists in a manner which later "Communist" tactics have made only too familiar. The equally familiar tactics of character-assassination were also resorted to by Marx, to his ever-lasting discredit, and Bakunin and his closest friend and collaborator, James Guillaume, were expelled from the International, the headquarters of which were at the same time shifted to New York to prevent it from falling into the hands of the anti-Marxists, who constituted a real majority in the International. That organisation soon withered and died in its alien home; but the Anarchists set up a new International in Switzerland and this lasted a few years more, surviving Bakunin himself.

It was based on Bakunin's idea of the Workers' International being a loose association of fully autonomous, national groups, devoted only to the economic struggle, in contradistinction to Marx's attempt to convert it into a highly centralised and rigidly controlled instrument of political manœuvres—in fact what Lenin afterwards made of the Third International.

In order to ventilate his grievances and to explain his attitude to Marx and Marxism, Bakunin wrote a lengthy letter to the Brussels newspaper *Liberté,* and large extracts from this letter have been printed in the following pages.

In 1873, Bakunin formally withdrew from political activities. His health had been permanently injured by the long years of solitary confinement in Russian prisons and, though he was a man of great size, physical strength and energy, he was now old before his time.

He came out of his retirement, however, for the last time, in May, 1874, to lead an insurrection in the Italian province of Bologna; but this was a complete fiasco. It had been meant as a political demonstration and this was in accordance with Bakunin's view that such actions should be used as a means of awakening the people's interest. He had had no faith whatever in the use of political action (in the sense of voting at Parliamentary elections and referenda) ever since the abortive revolutions of 1848 with their aftermath of betrayal of the workers and of democracy itself by the bourgeoisie. He agreed with Proudhon's dictum (born of the same events) that universal suffrage was counter-revolution.

His doctrine, however, had nothing in common with the Nihilistic tactics of bomb outrages and assassinations which, after his death, were adopted by some Anarchists and tended to discredit the movement. He believed in mass organisations, in solidarity, and to him Individualism was a bourgeois ideology—a mere excuse for egoism. True liberty could only be achieved in and through Society.

Bakunin was in other words a Socialist, or as he often called himself, a Collectivist, but his Socialism was of the Libertarian school and expressively rejected authority and, above all, the State. In this respect he followed the doctrine of Proudhon, not of Marx. His system in fact consists of Proudhonian politics and Marxian economics.

Bakunin died at Berne on 1st July, 1876, and was buried in the cemetery there. Exactly seventy years after his death, on the 1st July, 1946, a gathering of international Anarchists stood by his graveside to pay homage to his memory.

The message which, above all, Bakunin tried to preach was that only the workers could free the workers; in other words, he desired to stimulate the self-activity of the working-class. He was never tired of quoting the celebrated slogan of the First International: "The emancipation of the toilers must be the work of the toilers themselves," and he expressly excluded from the concept of "toilers" those ex-workers who, having gained the leadership of a working-class movement, endeavour to make themselves masters of it and lead it where they are determined that it shall go. To Bakunin that was not emancipation; it was merely a change of masters. But he wanted the triumph of Humanity—a concept he had borrowed from the great philosopher of Positivism, Auguste Comte—a full human development of all men in conditions of liberty and equality.

To him this could not be achieved by the methods envisaged by Marx and, in the pages that follow, he has given a picture of what he thought the Marxian State would be like. The startling similarity of this picture to that of present-day Soviet Russia is due to the fact that Lenin, the founder of the regime, himself a product of the despotic Tsarist regime, laid great stress on the authoritarian aspects of Marxism as opposed to the more democratic elements of Anarchism. Bakunin had assumed that, in practice, the authoritarian elements in Marxism when it attained power would predominate, and this turned out to be correct.

It is obvious of course that Marxism and Bakuninism despite these differences have much in common and Bakunin himself has not failed to point this out in the pages that follow. Both systems were founded on the idea of Historical Materialism, both accepted the class struggle, both were Socialist in the sense of being opposed to private property in the means of production. They differed in that Bakuninism refused to accept the State under any circumstances whatever, that it rejected Party politics or Parliamentary action, and that it was founded on the principle of liberty as against that of authority: and indeed, it is this spirit of liberty (not Individualism) that distinguishes Bakunin, and in the light of which his criticisms of Marx and Marxism must be read. He had the true instinct that no man can be really emancipated except by himself.

Up to the present, however, the emancipation of the workers has nowhere been achieved, either by Bakunin's methods nor by Marx's (and certainly not in Soviet Russia); but to-day the more militant elements in the Left-wing and anti-Stalinist Socialist movements are beginning to give Bakunin's teachings more serious consideration than Marxians had ever done before; and some of them are commencing to feel that after all there may be something in what he said. If, therefore, the Socialist movement, in its more militant and revolutionary aspects, continues to exist throughout the world, it is possible that the political theories of Marx may give way to those of Bakunin, and that in the end he will prevail as the inspiring genius of militant and democratic Socialism.

CHAPTER I

Introductory

I AM a passionate seeker after Truth and a not less passionate enemy of the malignant fictions used by the "Party of Order", the official representatives of all turpitudes, religious, metaphysical, political, judicial, economic, and social, present and past, to brutalise and enslave the world; I am a fanatical lover of Liberty; considering it as the only medium in which can develop intelligence, dignity, and the happiness of man; not official "Liberty", licensed, measured and regulated by the State, a falsehood representing the privileges of a few resting on the slavery of everybody else; not the individual liberty, selfish, mean, and fictitious advanced by the school of Rousseau and all other schools of bourgeois Liberalism, which considers the rights of the individual as limited by the rights of the State, and therefore necessarily results in the reduction of the rights of the individual to zero.

No, I mean the only liberty which is truly worthy of the name, the liberty which consists in the full development of all the material, intellectual and moral powers which are to be found as faculties latent in everybody, the liberty which recognises no other restrictions than those which are traced for us by the laws of our own nature; so that properly speaking there are no restrictions, since these laws are not imposed on us by some outside legislator, beside us or above us; they are immanent in us, inherent, constituting the very basis of our being, material as well as intellectual and moral; instead, therefore, of finding them a limit, we must consider them as the real conditions and effective reason for our liberty.

I mean that liberty of each individual which, far from halting as at a boundary before the liberty of others, finds there its confirmation and its extension to infinity; the illimitable liberty of each through the liberty of all, liberty by solidarity, liberty in equality;

liberty triumphing over brute force and the principle of authority which was never anything but the idealised expression of that force, liberty which, after having overthrown all heavenly and earthly idols, will found and organise a new world, that of human solidarity, on the ruins of all Churches and all States.

I am a convinced upholder of economic and social equality, because I know that, without that equality, liberty, justice, human dignity, morality, and the well-being of individuals as well as the prosperity of nations will never be anything else than so many lies. But as upholder in all circumstances of liberty, that first condition of humanity, I think that liberty must establish itself in the world by the spontaneous organisation of labour and of collective ownership by productive associations freely organised and federalised in districts, and by the equally spontaneous federation of districts, but not by the supreme and tutelary action of the State.

There is the point which principally divides the Revolutionary Socialists or Collectivists from the Authoritarian Communists, who are upholders of the absolute initiative of the State. Their goal is the same; each party desires equally the creation of a new social order founded only on the organisation of collective labour, inevitably imposed on each and everyone by the very force of things, equal economic conditions for all, and the collective appropriation of the instruments of labour. Only, the Communists imagine that they will be able to get there by the development and organisation of the political power of the working-classes, and principally of the pro-letariat of the towns, by the help of the bourgeois Radicalism, whilst the Revolutionary Socialists, enemies of all equivocal combinations and alliances, think on the contrary that they cannot reach this goal except by the development and organisation, not of the political but of the social and consequently anti-political power of the working masses of town and country alike, including all favourably disposed persons of the upper classes, who, breaking completely with their past, would be willing to join them and fully accept their programme.

Hence, two different methods. The Communists believe they must organise the workers' forces to take possession of the political power of the State. The Revolutionary Socialists organise with a view to the destruction, or if you prefer a politer word, the liquidation of the State. The Communists are the upholders of the principle and practice of authority, the Revolutionary Socialists have confidence only in liberty. Both equally supporters of that science which must kill superstition and replace faith, the former would wish to impose it; the latter will exert themselves to propagate it so that groups of human beings, convinced, will organise themselves and will federate spontaneously, freely, from below upwards, by their own movement and conformably to their real interests, but never after a plan traced in advance and imposed on the "ignorant masses" by some superior intellects.

The Revolutionary Socialists think that there is much more practical sense and spirit in the instinctive aspirations and in the real needs of the masses of the people than in the profound intellect of all these learned men and tutors of humanity who, after so many efforts have failed to make it happy, still presume to add their efforts. The Revolutionary Socialists think, on the contrary, that the human race has let itself long enough, too long, be governed, and that the source of its misfortunes does not lie in such or such form of government but in the very principle and fact of government, of whatever type it may be. It is, in fine, the contradiction already become historic, which exists between the Communism scientifically developed by the German school[1] and accepted in part by the American and English Socialists on the one hand, and the Proudhonism largely developed and pushed to its last consequences, on the other hand, which is accepted by the proletariat of the Latin countries.

It has equally been accepted and will continue to be still more accepted by the essentially anti-political sentiment of the Slav peoples.

---

1 That is, the Marxians.

CHAPTER II

Marxist Ideology

THE doctrinaire school of Socialists, or rather of German Authoritarian Communists, was founded a little before 1848, and has rendered, it must be recognised, eminent services to the cause of the proletariat not only in Germany, but in Europe. It is to them that belongs principally the great idea of an "International Working-men's Association" and also the initiative for its first realisation. To-day,[2] they are to be found at the head of the Social Democratic Labour Party in Germany, having as its organ the "Volksstaat" ["People's State"].

It is therefore a perfectly respectable school which does not prevent it from displaying a very bad disposition sometimes, and above all from taking for the bases of its theories, a principal[3] which is profoundly true when one considers it in its true light, that is to say, from the relative point of view, but which when envisaged and set down in an absolute manner as the only foundation and first source of all other principles, as is done by this school, becomes completely false.

This principle, which constitutes besides the essential basis of scientific Socialism, was for the first time scientifically formulated and developed by Karl Marx, the principal leader of the German Communist school. It forms the dominating thought of the celebrated "Communist Manifesto" which an international Committee of French, English, Belgian and German Communists assembled in London issued in 1848 under the slogan: "Proletarians of all lands, unite!" This manifesto, drafted as everyone knows, by Messrs. Marx and Engels, became the basis of all the further scientific works of the

---

2 i.e., 1871.
3 Historical Materialism.

school and of the popular agitation later started by Ferdinand Lassalle[4] in Germany.

This principle is the absolute opposite to that recognised by the Idealists of all schools. Whilst these latter derive all historical facts, including the development of material interests and of the different phases of the economic organisation of society, from the development of Ideas, the German Communists, on the contrary, want to see in all human history, in the most idealistic manifestations of the collective as well as the individual life of humanity, in all the intellecual, moral, religious, metaphysical, scientific, artistic, political, juridical, and social developments which have been produced in the past and continue to be produced in the present, nothing but the reflections or the necessary after-effects of the development of economic facts. Whilst the Idealists maintain that ideas dominate and produce facts, the Communists, in agreement besides with scientific Materialism say, on the contrary, that facts give birth to ideas and that these latter are never anything else but the ideal expression of accomplished facts and that among all the facts, economic and material facts, the pre-eminent facts, constitute the essential basis, the principal foundation of which all the other facts, intellectual and moral, political and social, are nothing more than the inevitable derivatives.

We, who are Materialists and Determinists, just as much as Marx himself, we also recognise the inevitable linking of economic and political facts in history. We recognise, indeed, the necessity, the inevitable character of all events that happen, but we do not bow before them indifferently and above all we are very careful about praising them when, by their nature, they show themselves in flagrant opposition to the supreme end of history[5] to the thoroughly human

---

4 Lassalle lived 1825–64; a brilliant demagogue, he popularised (or vulgarised) Marx's teachings and launched the Social Democratic Movement in Germany. His organisation, the General Association of German Workers, united with the Marxists in 1845.

5 Bakunin's use of the term "supreme end of history" (in the sense of aim or objective), must not be taken to have a teleological signification, that is, taken to mean that he considered that the nature of things is such that there is a cosmic aim or purpose which informs the whole cosmic activity. Such a theory inevitably involves the notion of some directive intelligence behind Nature, and this, as a materialist, Bakunin absolutely denied.

He means by "supreme end of history" simply the ideal at which the human race should aim, as defined by him a few lines further on in

ideal that is to be found under more or less obvious forms, in the instincts, the aspirations of the people and under all the religious symbols of all epochs, because it is inherent in the human race, the most social of all the races of animals on earth. Thus this ideal, to-day better understood than ever, can be summed up in the words: It is *the triumph of humanity, it is the conquest and accomplishment of the full freedom and full development, material, intellectual and moral, of every individual, by the absolutely free and spontaneous organisation of economic and social solidarity as completely as possible between all human beings living on the earth.*

Everything in history that shows itself conformable to that end, from the human point of view—and we can have no other—is good; all that is contrary to it is bad. We know very well, in any case, that what we call good and bad are always, one and the other, the natural results of natural causes, and that consequently one is as inevitable as the other. But as in what is properly called Nature we recognise many necessities that we are little disposed to bless, for example the necessity of dying of hydrophobia when bitten by a mad dog,[6] in the same way, in that immediate continuation of the life of Nature, called History, we encounter many necessities which we find much more worthy of opprobrium than of benediction and which we believe we should stigmatise with all the energy of which we are capable, in the interest of our social and individual morality, although we recognise that from the moment they have been accomplished, even the most detestable historic facts have that character of inevitability which is found in all the phenomena of Nature as well as those of history.

To make my idea clearer, I shall illustrate it by some examples. When I study the respective social and political conditions in which the Romans and the Greeks came into contact towards the decline

---

the text. As he said in another passage of his works, man is part of universal Nature and cannot fight against it; "But by studying its laws, by identifying himself in some sort with them, transforming them by a psychological process proper to his brain, into ideas and human convictions, he emancipates himself from the triple yoke imposed on him firstly by external Nature, then by his own individual inward Nature, and finally by the society of which he is the product." (*Michael Bakunin and Karl Marx*, p. 337.)

6 Bakunin wrote some years before Pasteur's discovery of a cure for this disease.

of Antiquity, I arrive at the conclusion that the conquest and des-truction by the military and civic barbarism of the Romans, of the comparatively high standard of human liberty of Greece was a logical, natural, absolutely inevitable fact. But that does not prevent me at all from taking retrospectively and very firmly, the side of Greece against Rome in that struggle, and I find that the human race gained absolutely nothing by the triumph of the Romans.

In the same way, I consider as perfectly natural, logical, and consequently inevitable fact, that Christians should have destroyed with a holy fury all the libraries of the Pagans, all the treasures of Art, and of ancient philosophy and science.[7] But it is absolutely impossible for me to grasp what advantages have resulted from it for our political and social development. I am even very much disposed to think that apart from that inevitable process of economic facts in which, if one were to believe Marx, there must be sought to the exclusion of all other considerations, the only cause of all the intellectual and moral facts which are produced in history—I say I am strongly disposed to think that this act of holy barbarity, or rather that long series of barbarous acts and crimes which the first Christians, divinely inspired, committed against the human spirit, was one of the principal causes of the intellectual and moral degradation and consequently also of the political and social enslavement which filled that long series of baneful centuries called the Middle Ages. Be sure of this, that if the first Christians had not destroyed the libraries, Museums, and Temples of antiquity, we should not have been condemned to-day to fight the mass of horrible and shameful absurdities, which still obstruct men's brains to such a degree as to make us doubt sometimes the possibility of a more human future.

Following on with the same order of protests against facts which have happened in history and of which consequently I myself recognise the inevitable character, I pause before the splendour of the Italian Republics and before the magnificent awakening of human genius in the epoch of the Renaissance. Then I see approaching the two

---

7 This, of course, is an exaggeration on Bakunin's part. Such vandalism was not common. It was the political convulsions, barbarian invasions, and endless wars, foreign and civil, that caused the decline of culture. The Christians tended to neglect and ignore the classical culture rather than persecute it. Of course, it is true that the decline and practical extinction of the ancient culture greatly impaired intellectual progress.

evil geniuses, as ancient as history itself, the two boa-constrictors which up till now have devoured everything human and beautiful that history has produced. They are called the Church and the State, the *Papacy* and the *Empire*. Eternal evils and inseparable allies, I see them become reconciled, embrace each other and together devour and stifle and crush that unfortunate and too beautiful Italy, condemn her to three centuries of death. Well, again I find all that very natural, logical, inevitable, but nevertheless abominable, and I curse both Pope and Emperor at the same time.

Let us pass on to France. After a struggle which lasted a century Catholicism, supported by the State, finally triumphed there over Protestantism. Well, do I not still find in France to-day some politicians or historians of the fatalist school and who, calling themselves Revolutionaries, consider this victory of Catholicism—a bloody and inhuman victory if ever there was one—as a veritable triumph for the Revolution? Catholicism, they maintain, was then the State, democracy, whilst Protestantism represented the revolt of the aristocracy against the State and consequently against democracy. It is with sophisms like that—completely identical besides with the Marxian sophisms, which, also, consider the triumphs of the State as those of Social Democracy—it is with these absurdities, as disgusting as revolting, that the mind and moral sense of the masses is perverted, habituating them to consider their blood-thirsty exploiters, their age-long enemies, their tyrants, the masters and the servants of the State, as the organs, representatives, heroes, devoted servants of their emancipation.

It is a thousand times right to say that Protestantism then, not as Calvinist theology, but as an energetic and armed protest, represented revolt, liberty, humanity, the destruction of the State; whilst Catholicism was public order, authority, divine law, the salvation of the State by the Church and the Church by the State, the condemnation of human society to a boundless and endless slavery.

Whilst recognising the inevitability of the accomplished fact, I do not hesitate to say that the triumph of Catholicism in France in the sixteenth and seventeenth centuries was a great misfortune for the whole human race, and that the massacre of Saint Bartholomew, as well as the Revocation of the Edict of Nantes, were facts as disastrous for France herself as were lately the defeat and massacre of the people of Paris in the Commune. I have actually heard very intelligent and very estimable Frenchmen explain this defeat of Protestantism in France by the essentially revolutionary nature of the French people. "Protestantism," they said, "was only a semi-revolution; we needed a complete revolution; it is for that reason that the French nation did not wish, and was not able to stop at the Reformation. It preferred to remain Catholic till the moment when it could proclaim Atheism; and it is because of that that it bore with such a perfect and Christian resignation both the horrors of Saint Bartholomew and those not less abominable of the executors of the Revocation of the Edict of Nantes."

These estimable patriots do not seem to want to consider one thing. It is that a people, who under whatsoever pretext it may be, suffers tyranny, necessarily loses at length the salutory habit of revolt and even the very instinct of revolt. It loses the feeling for liberty, and once a people has lost all that, it necessarily becomes not only by its outer conditions, but in itself, in the very essence of its being, a people of slaves. It was because Protestantism was defeated in France that the French people lost, or rather, never acquired, the custom of liberty. It is because this tradition and this custom are lacking in it that it has not to-day what we call *political conscious-ness*, and it is because it is lacking in this consciousness that all the revolutions it has made up to now have not been able to give it or secure it political liberty. With the exception of its great revolutionary days, which are its festival days, the French people remain to-day as yesterday, a people of slaves.

CHAPTER III

The State and Marxism

ALL work to be performed in the employ and pay of the State—such is the fundamental principle of Authoritarian Communism, of State Socialism. The State having become sole proprietor—at the end of a certain period of transition which will be necessary to let society pass without too great political and economic shocks from the present organisation of bourgeois privilege to the future organisation of the official equality of all—the State will be also the only Capitalist, banker, money-lender, organiser, director of all national labour and distributor of its products. Such is the ideal, the fundamental principle of modern Communism.

Enunciated for the first time by Babeuf,[8] towards the close of the Great French Revolution, with all the array of antique civism and revolutionary violence, which constituted the character of the epoch, it was recast and reproduced in miniature, about forty-five years later by Louis Blanc[9] in his tiny pamphlet on *The Organisation of Labour*, in which that estimable citizen, much less revolutionary, and much more indulgent towards bourgeois weaknesses than was Babeuf, tried to gild and sweeten the pill so that the bourgeois could swallow it without suspecting that they were taking a poison which would kill them. But the bourgeois were not deceived, and returning brutality for politeness, they expelled Louis Blanc from France. In spite of that, with a constancy which one must admire, he remained alone in faithfulness to his economic system and continued to believe that the whole future was contained in his little pamphlet on the organisation of Labour.

8 Babeuf (1762–97) formed conspiracy of "Equals" to seize power in France and introduce an authoritarian equalitarian Communism. Plot discovered and conspirators executed.

9 Blanc, Louis (1811–82) advocated State Socialism in France, particularly in the period 1840–50.

The Communist idea later passed into more serious hands. Karl Marx, the undisputed chief of the Socialist Party in Germany—a great intellect armed with a profound knowledge, whose entire life, one can say it without flattering, has been devoted exclusively to the greatest cause which exists to-day, the emancipation of labour and of the toilers—Karl Marx who is indisputably also, if not the only, at least one of the principal founders of the International Workingmen's Association, made the development of the Communist idea the object of a serious work. His great work, *Capital,* is not in the least a fantasy, an "a priori" conception, hatched out in a single day in the head of a young man more or less ignorant of economic conditions and of the actual system of production. It is founded on a very extensive, very detailed knowledge and a very profound analysis of this system and of its conditions. Karl Marx is a man of immense statistical and economic knowledge. His work on Capital, though unfortunately bristling with formulas and metaphysical subtleties, which render it unapproachable for the great mass of readers, is in the highest degree a scientific or realist work: in the sense that it absolutely excludes any other logic than that of the facts.

Living for very nearly thirty years, almost exclusively among German workers, refugees like himself and surrounded by more or less intelligent friends and disciples belonging by birth and relationship to the bourgeois world, Marx naturally has managed to form a Communist school, or a sort of little Communist Church, composed of fervent adepts and spread all over Germany. This Church, restricted though it may be on the score of numbers, is skilfully organised, and thanks to its numerous connections with working-class organisations in all the principal places in Germany, it has already become a power.[10] Karl Marx naturally enjoys an almost supreme authority in this Church, and to do him justice, it must be admitted that he knows how to govern this little army of fanatical adherents in such a way as always to enhance his prestige and power over the imagination of the workers of Germany.

Marx is not only a learned Socialist, he is also a very clever politician and an ardent patriot. Like Bismarck, though by somewhat

10 Written in September, 1870.

different means, and like many other of his compatriots, Socialists or not, he wants the establishment of a great Germanic State for the glory of the German people and for the happiness and the voluntary, or enforced civilisation of the world.

The policy of Bismarck is that of the present; the policy of Marx, who considers himself at least as his successor, and his continuator, is that of the future. And when I say that Marx considers himself the continuator of Bismarck, I am far from calumniating Marx. If he did not consider himself as such, he would not have permitted Engels, the confidant of all his thoughts, to write that Bismarck serves the cause of Social Revolution. He serves it now in his own way; Marx will serve it later, in another manner. That is the sense in which he will be later, the continuator, as to-day he is the admirer of the policy of Bismarck.

Now let us examine the particular character of Marx's policy, let us ascertain the essential points on which it is to be separated from the Bismarckian policy. The principal point, and, one might say, the only one, is this: Marx is a democrat, an Authoritarian Socialist, and a Republican; Bismarck is an out and out Pomeranian, aristocratic, monarchical Junker. The difference is therefore very great, very serious, and both sides are sincere in this difference. On this point, there is no possible understanding or reconciliation possible between Bismarck and Marx. Even apart from the numerous irrevocable pledges that Marx throughout his life, has given to the cause of Socialist democracy, his very position and his ambitions give a positive guarantee on this issue. In a monarchy, however Liberal it might be, or even cannot be any place, any rôle for Marx, and so much the more so in the Prussian Germanic Empire founded by Bismarck, with a bugbear of an Emperor, militarist and bigoted, as chief and with all the barons and bureaucrats of Germany for guardians. Before he can arrive at power, Marx will have to sweep all that away.

Therefore he is forced to be Revolutionary. That is what separates Marx from Bismarck—the form and the conditions of Government. One is an out and out aristocrat and monarchist; and in a Conservative Republic like that of France under Thiers,[11] there

---

11 Thiers, Adolphe (1797–1877), President of the Third Republic in 1871-3. He was primarily responsible for the ruthless suppression of the Paris Commune.

the other is an out and out democrat and republican, and, into the bargain, a Socialist democrat and a Socialist republican.

Let us see now what unites them. *It is the out and out cult of the State.* I have no need to prove it in the case of Bismarck, the proofs are there. From head to foot he is a State's man and nothing but a State's man. But neither do I believe that I shall have need of too great efforts to prove that it is the same with Marx. He loves government to such a degree that he even wanted to institute one in the International Workingmen's Association; and he worships power so much that he wanted to impose and still means to-day to impose his dictatorship on us. It seems to me that that is sufficient to characterise his personal attitude. But his Socialist and political programme is a very faithful expression of it. The supreme objective of all his efforts, as is proclaimed to us by the fundamental statutes of his party in Germany, is the establishment of the great People's State (Volksstaat).

But whoever says State, necessarily says a particular limited State, doubtless comprising, if it is very large, many different peoples and countries, but excluding still more. For unless he is dreaming of the Universal State, as did Napoleon and the Emperor Charles the Fifth, or as the Papacy dreamed of the Universal Church, Marx, in spite of all the international ambition which devours him to-day, will have, when the hour of the realisation of his dreams has sounded for him—if it ever does sound—he will have to content himself with governing a single State and not several States at once. Consequently, who ever says State says, *a* State, and whoever says *a* State affirms by that the existence of several States, and whoever says *several* States, immediately says: competition, jealousy, truceless and endless war. The simplest logic as well as all history bear witness to it.

Any State, under pain of perishing and seeing itself devoured by neighbouring States, must tend towards complete power, and, having become powerful, it must embark on a career of conquest, so that it shall not be itself conquered; for two powers similar and at the same time foreign to each other could not co-exist without trying to destroy each other. Whoever says conquest, says conquered peoples, enslaved and in bondage, under whatever form or name it may be.

It is in the nature of the State to break the solidarity of the human race and, as it were, to deny humanity. The State cannot preserve itself as such in its integrity and in all its strength except it sets itself up as supreme and absolute be-all and end-all, at least for its own citizens, or to speak more frankly, for its own subjects, not being able to impose itself as such on the citizens of other States unconquered by it. From that there inevitably results a break with human, considered as universal, morality and with universal reason, by the birth of State morality and reasons of State. The principle of political or State morality is very simple. The State, being the supreme objective, everything that is favourable to the development of its power is good; all that is contrary to it, even if it were the most humane thing in the world, is bad. This morality is called *Patriotism*. The International is the negation of patriotism and consequently the negation of the State. If therefore Marx and his friends of the German Socialist Democratic Party should succeed in introducing the State principle into our programme, they would kill the International.

The State, for its own preservation, must necessarily be powerful as regards foreign affairs; but if it is so as regards foreign affairs, it will infallibly be so as regards home affairs. Every State, having to let itself be inspired and directed by some particular morality, conformable to the particular conditions of its existence, by a morality which is a restriction and consequently a negation of human and universal morality, must keep watch that all its subjects, in their thoughts and above all in their acts, are inspired also only by the principles of this patriotic or particular morality, and that they remain deaf to the teachings of pure or universally human morality. From that there results the necessity for a State censorship; too great liberty of thought and opinions being, as Marx considers, very reasonably too from his eminently political point of view, incompatible with that unanimity of adherence demanded by the security of the State. That that in reality is Marx's opinion is sufficiently proved by the attempts which he made to introduce censorship into the International, under plausible pretexts, and covering it with a mask.

But however vigilant this censorship may be, even if the State were to take into its own hands exclusively education and all the instruction of the people, as Mazzini wished to do, and as Marx wishes to do to-day, the State can never be sure that prohibited and dangerous thoughts may not slip in and be smuggled somehow into the consciousness of the population that it governs. Forbidden fruit has such an attraction for men, and the demon of revolt, that eternal enemy of the State, awakens so easily in their hearts when they are not sufficiently stupified, that neither this education nor this instruction, nor even the censorship, sufficiently guarantee the tranquillity of the State. It must still have a police, devoted agents who watch over and direct, secretly and unobstrusively, the current of the peoples' opinions and passions. We have seen that Marx himself is so convinced of this necessity, that he believed he should fill with his secret agents all the regions of the International and above all, Italy, France, and Spain. Finally, however perfect may be, from the point of view of the preservation of the State, the organisation of education and instruction for the people, of censorship and the police, the State cannot be secure in its existence while it does not have, to defend it against its *enemies at home,* an armed force. The State is government from above downwards of an immense number of men, very different from the point of view of the degree of their culture, the nature of the countries or localities that they inhabit, the occupation they follow, the interests and the aspirations directing them—the State is the government of all these by some or other minority; this minority, even if it were a thousand times elected by universal suffrage and controlled in its acts by popular institutions, unless it were endowed with the omniscience, omnipresence and the omnipotence which the theologians attribute to God, it is impossible that it could know and foresee the needs, or satisfy with an even justice the most legitimate and pressing interests in the world. There will always be discontented people because there will always be some who are sacrificed.

Besides, the State, like the Church, by its very nature is a great sacrificer of living beings. It is an arbitrary being, in whose heart all the positive, living, individual, and local interests of the population meet, clash, destroy each other, become absorbed in that abstraction called the common interest, the *public good,* the *public safety,* and where all real wills cancel each other in that other abstraction which bears the name of the *will of the people*. It results from this, that this so-called will of the people is never anything else than the sacrifice and the negation of all the real wills of the population; just as this so-called public good is nothing else than the sacrifice of their interests. But so that this omnivorous abstraction could impose itself on millions of men, it must be represented and supported by some real being, by some living force or other. Well, this being, this force, has always existed. In the Church it is called the clergy, and in the State—the ruling or governing class.

And, in fact, what do we find throughout history? The State has always been the patrimony of some privileged class or other; a priestly class, an aristocratic class, a bourgeois class, and finally a bureaucratic class, when, all the other classes having become exhausted, the State falls or rises, as you will, to the condition of a machine; but it is absolutely necessary for the salvation of the State that there should be some privileged class or other which is interested in its existence. And it is precisely the united interest of this privileged class which is called Patriotism.

By excluding the immense majority of the human race from its bosom, by casting it beyond the pale of the engagements and reciprocal duties of morality, justice and right, the State denies humanity, and with that big word, "Patriotism", imposes injustice and cruelty on all its subjects, as a supreme duty. It restrains, it mutilates, it kills humanity in them, so that, ceasing to be men, they are no longer anything but citizens—or rather, more correctly considered in relation to the historic succession of facts—so that they shall never raise themselves beyond the level of the citizen to the level of a man.

If we accept the fiction of a free State derived from a social contract, then discerning, just, prudent people ought not to have any longer any need of government or of State. Such a people can need only to live, leaving a free course to all their instincts: justice and public order will naturally and of their accord proceed from the life of the people, and the State, ceasing to be the providence, guide, educator, and regulator of society, renouncing all its repressive power, and falling to the subaltern rôle which Proudhon assigns it, will no longer be anything else but a simple business office, a sort of central clearing house at the service of society.

Doubtless, such a political organisation, or rather, such a reduction of political action in favour of liberty in social life, would be a great benefit for society, but it would not at all please the devoted adherents of the State. They absolutely must have a State-Providence, a State directing social life, dispensing justice, and administering public order. That is to say, whether they admit it or not, and even when they call themselves Republicans, democrats, or even Socialists, they always must have a people who are more or less ignorant, minor, incapable, or to call things by their right names, riff-raff, to govern; in order, of course, that doing violence to their own disinterestedness and modesty, they can keep the best places for themselves, in order always to have the opportunity to devote themselves to the common good, and that, strong in their virtuous devotion and their exclusive intelligence, privileged guardians of the human flock, whilst urging it on for its own good and leading it to security, they may also fleece it a little.

Every logical and sincere theory of the State is essentially founded on the principle of *authority*—that is to say on the eminently theological, metaphysical and political idea that the masses, *always* incapable of governing themselves, must submit at all times to the benevolent yoke of a wisdom and a justice, which in one way or another, is imposed on them from above. But imposed in the name of what and by whom? Authority recognised and respected as such by the masses can have only three possible sources—force, religion, or the action of a superior intelligence; and this supreme intelligence is always represented by minorities.

Slavery can change its form and its name—its basis remains the same. This basis is expressed by the words: being a slave is being forced to work for other people—as being a master is to live on the labour of other people. In ancient times, as to-day in Asia and Africa, slaves were simply called slaves. In the Middle Ages, they took the name of "serfs", to-day they are called "wage-earners". The position of these latter is much more honourable and less hard than that of slaves, but they are none the less forced by hunger as well as by the political and social institutions, to maintain by very

33

hard work the absolute or relative idleness of others. Consequently, they are slaves. And, in general, no State, either ancient or modern, has ever been able, or ever will be able to do without the forced labour of the masses, whether wage-earners or slaves, as a principal and absolutely necessary basis of the liberty and culture of the political class: the citizens.

Even the United States is no exception to this rule. Its marvellous prosperity and enviable progress are due in great part and above all to one important advantage—the great territorial wealth of North America. The immense quantity of uncultivated and fertile lands, together with a political liberty that exists nowhere else attracts every year hundreds of thousands of energetic, industrious and intelligent colonists. This wealth, at the same time keeps off pauperism and delays the moment when the social question will have to be put. A worker who does not find work or who is dissatisfied with the wages offered by the capitalist can always, if need be, emigrate to the far West to clear there some wild and unoccupied land.[12]

This possibility always remaining open as a last resort to all American workers, naturally keeps wages at a level, and gives to every individual an independence, unknown in Europe. Such is the advantage, but here is the disadvantage. As cheapness of the products of industry is achieved in great part by cheapness of labour, the American manufacturers for most of the time are not in a condition to compete against the manufacturers of Europe—from which there results, for the industry of the Northern States, the necessity for a protectionist tariff. But that has a result, firstly to create a host of artificial industries and above all to oppress and ruin the non-manufacturing Southern States and make them want secession; finally to crowd together into cities like New York, Philadelphia, Boston and many others, proletarian working masses who, little by little, are beginning to find themselves already in a situation analogous to that of the workers in the great manufacturing

12 It should be kept in mind in reading this and the following paragraphs concerning the United States, that they were written in 1867, not long after the close of the Civil War. At that time it was not as easy to see as it is now, that the Republican Party was not really a "Party of Liberation" but the Party of Industrial Capitalism, and that the Civil War was fought, not to "emancipate the slaves" but merely to decide whether they should continue as chattel slaves, or change their status to that of wage-slaves.

States of Europe. And we see, in effect, the social question already being posed in the Northern States, just as it was posed long before in our countries.

And there too, the self-government of the masses, in spite of all the display of the people's omnipotence, remains most of the time in a state of fiction. In reality, it is minorities which govern. The so-called Democratic Party, up to the time of the Civil War to emancipate the slaves, were the out and out partisans of slavery and of the ferocious oligarchy of the planters, demagogues without faith or conscience, capable of sacrificing everything to their greed and evil-minded ambition, and who, by their detestable influence and actions, exercised almost unhindered, for nearly fifty years continuously, have greatly contributed to deprave the political morality of North America.

The Republican Party, though really intelligent and generous, is still and always a minority, and whatever the sincerity of this party of liberation, however great and generous the principles it professes, do not let us hope that, in power, it will renounce this exclusive position of a governing minority to merge into the mass of the nation so that the self-government of the people shall finally become a reality. For that there will be necessary a revolution far more profound than all those which hitherto have shaken the Old and New Worlds.

In Switzerland, in spite of all the democratic revolutions that have taken place there, it is still always the class in comfortable circumstances, the bourgeoisie, that is to say, the class privileged by wealth, leisure, and education, which governs. The sovereignty of the people—a word which, anyway, we detest because in our eyes, all sovereignty is detestable—the government of the people by themselves is likewise a fiction. The people is sovereign in law, not in fact, for necessarily absorbed by their daily labour, which leaves them no leisure, and if not completely ignorant, at least very inferior in education to the bourgeoisie, they are forced to place in the hands of the latter their supposed sovereignty. The sole advantage which they get out of it in Switzerland, as in the United

States, is that ambitious minorities, the political classes, cannot arrive at power otherwise than by paying court to the people, flattering their fleeting passions, which may sometimes be very bad, and most often deceiving them.

It is true that the most imperfect republic is a thousand times better than the most enlightened monarchy, for at least in the republic there are moments when, though always exploited, the people are not oppressed, while in monarchies they are never anything else. And then the democratic regime trains the masses little by little in public life, which the monarchy never does. But whilst giving the preference to the republic we are nevertheless forced to recognise and proclaim that whatever may be the form of government, whilst human society remains divided into different classes because of the hereditary inequality of occupations, wealth, education, and privileges, there will always be minority government and the inevitable exploitation of the majority by that minority.

The State is nothing else but this domination and exploitation regularised and systematised. We shall attempt to demonstrate it by examining the consequence of the government of the masses of the people by a minority, at first as intelligent and as devoted as you like, in an ideal State, founded on a free contract.

Suppose the government to be confined only to the best citizens. At first these citizens are privileged not by right, but by fact. They have been elected by the people because they are the most intelligent, clever, wise, and courageous and devoted. Taken from the mass of the citizens, who are regarded as all equal, they do not yet form a class apart, but a group of men privileged only by nature and for that very reason singled out for election by the people. Their number is necessarily very limited, for in all times and countries the number of men endowed with qualities so remarkable that they automatically command the unanimous respect of a nation is, as experience teaches us, very small. Therefore, under pain of making a bad choice, the people will be always forced to choose its rulers from amongst them.

Here, then, is society divided into two categories, if not yet to say two classes, of which one, composed of the immense majority of the citizens, submits freely to the government of its elected leaders, the other, formed of a small number of privileged natures, recognised and accepted as such by the people, and charged by them to govern them. Dependent on popular election, they are at first distinguished from the mass of the citizens only by the very qualities which recommended them to their choice and are naturally, the most devoted and useful of all. They do not yet assume to themselves any privilege, any particular right, except that of exercising, insofar as the people wish it, the special functions with which they have been charged. For the rest, by their manner of life, by the conditions and means of their existence, they do not separate themselves in any way from all the others, so that a perfect equality continues to reign among all. Can this equality be long maintained? We claim that it cannot and nothing is easier to prove it.

Nothing is more dangerous for man's private morality than the habit of command. The best man, the most intelligent, disinterested, generous, pure, will infallibly and always be spoiled at this trade. Two sentiments inherent in power never fail to produce this demoralisation; they are: contempt for the masses and the overestimation of one's own merits.

"The masses," a man says to himself, "recognising their incapacity to govern on their own account, have elected me their chief. By that act they have publicly proclaimed their inferiority and my superiority. Among this crowd of men, recognising hardly any equals of myself, I am alone capable of directing public affairs. The people have need of me; they cannot do without my services, while I, on the contrary, can get along all right by myself: they, therefore, must obey me for their own security, and in condescending to command them, I am doing them a good turn."

Is not there something in all that to make a man lose his head and his heart as well, and become mad with pride? It is thus that power and the habit of command become for even the most intelligent and virtuous men, a source of aberration, both intellectual and moral.

But in the People's State of Marx, there will be, we are told, no privileged class at all. All will be equal, not only from the juridical and political point of view, but from the economic point of view. At least that is what is promised, though I doubt very much, considering the manner in which it is being tackled and the course it is desired to follow, whether that promise could ever be kept. There will therefore be no longer any privileged class, but there will be a government, and, note this well, an extremely complex government, which will not content itself with governing and administering the masses politically, as all governments do to-day, but which will also administer them economically, concentrating in its own hands the production and the just division of wealth, the cultivation of land, the establishment and development of factories, the organisation and direction of commerce, finally the application of capital to production by the only banker, the State. All that will demand an immense knowledge and many "heads overflowing with brains"[13] in this government. It will be the reign of *scientific intelligence*, the most aristocratic, despotic, arrogant and contemptuous of all regimes. There will be a new class, a new hierarchy of real and pretended scientists and scholars, and the world will be divided into a minority ruling in the name of knowledge and an immense ignorant majority.[14] And then, woe betide the mass of ignorant ones!

Such a regime will not fail to arouse very considerable discontent in this mass and in order to keep it in check the enlightenment and liberating government of Marx will have need of a not less considerable armed force. For the government must be strong, says Engels, to maintain order among these millions of illiterates whose brutal uprising would be capable of destroying and overthrowing everything, even a government directed by heads overflowing with brains.

You can see quite well that behind all the democratic and socialistic phrases and promises of Marx's programme, there is to be found in his State all that constitutes the true despotic and brutal nature of all States, whatever may be the form of their government and that in the final reckoning, the People's State so strongly commended by Marx, and the aristocratic-monarchic State, maintained with as much cleverness as power by Bismarck, are completely identical by the nature of their objective at home as well as in foreign affairs. In foreign affairs it is the same deployment of military force, that is to say, conquest; and in home affairs it is the same employment of this armed force, the last argument of all threatened political

---

13 A satiric allusion to the reference to Marx by Sorge, the German-American delegate, at the Hague Conference.

14 Compare James Burnham's theory in his *Managerial Revolution*.

powers against the masses, who, tired of believing, hoping, submitting and obeying always, rise in revolt.

Marx's Communist idea comes to light in all his writings; it is also manifest in the motions put forward by the General Council of the International Workingmen's Association, situated in London, at the Congress of Basel in 1869, as well as by the proposals which he had intended to present to the Congress which was to take place in September, 1870, but which had to be suspended because of the Franco-German War. As a member of the General Council in London and as corresponding Secretary for Germany, Marx enjoys in this Council, as is well known, a great and it must be admitted, legitimate influence, so that it can be taken for certain that of the motions put to the Congress by the Council, several are principally derived from the system and the collaboration of Marx. It was in this way that the English citizen Lucraft, a member of the General Council, put forward at the Congress of Basel the idea that all the land in a country should become the property of the State, and that the cultivation of this land should be directed and administered by State officials, "Which," he added, "will only be possible in a democratic and Socialist State, in which the people will have to watch carefully over the good administration of the national land by the State."

This cult of the State is, in general, the principal characteristic of German Socialism. Lassalle, the greatest Socialist agitator and the true founder of the practical Socialist movement in Germany was steeped in it. He saw no salvation for the workers except in the power of the State; of which the workers should possess themselves, according to him, by means of universal suffrage.

CHAPTER IV

Internationalism
and the State

LET us consider the real, national policy of Marx himself. Like Bismarck, he is a German patriot. He desires the greatness and power of Germany as a State. No one anyway will count it a crime in him to love his country and his people; and since he is so profoundly convinced that the State is the condition *sine qua non* of the prosperity of the one and the emancipation of the other, it will be found natural that he should desire to see Germany organised into a very large and very powerful State, since weak and small States always run the risk of seeing themselves swallowed up. Consequently Marx as a clear-sighted and ardent patriot, must wish for the greatness and strength of Germany as a State.

But, on the other hand, Marx is a celebrated Socialist and, what is more, one of the principal initiators of the International. He does not content himself with working for the emancipation of the proletariat of Germany alone; he feels himself in honour bound, and he considers it as his duty, to work at the same time for the emancipation of the proletariat of all other countries; the result is that he finds himself in complete conflict with himself. As a German patriot, he wants the greatness and power, that is to say, the domination of Germany; but as a Socialist of the International he must wish for the emancipation of all the peoples of the world. How can this contradiction be resolved?

There is only one way, that is to proclaim, after he has persuaded himself of it, of course, that the greatness and power of Germany as a State, is a supreme condition of the emancipation of the whole world, that the national and political triumph of Germany, is the triumph of humanity, and that all that is contrary to the advent of this great new omnivorous power is the enemy of humanity.

This conviction once established, it is not only permitted, but it is commanded by the most sacred of causes, to make the International, including all the Federations of other countries, serve as a very powerful, convenient, above all, popular means for the setting up of the great Pan-German State. And that is precisely what Marx tried to do, as much by the deliberations of the Conference he called at London in 1871 as by the resolutions voted by his German and French friends at the Hague Congress. If he did not succeed better, it is assuredly not for lack of very great efforts and much skill on his part, but probably because the fundamental idea which inspires him is false and its realization is impossible.

One cannot commit a greater mistake than to ask either of a thing or of an institution, or of a man more than they can give. By demanding more from them one demoralises, impedes, perverts and kills them. The International in a short time produced great results. It organised and it will organise every day in a more formidable manner still, the proletariat for the economic struggle. Is that a reason to hope that one can use it as an instrument for the political struggle? Marx, because he thought so, very nearly killed the International, by his criminal attempt at the Hague. It is the story of the goose with the golden eggs. At the summons to the economic struggle masses of workers of different countries hastened along to range themselves under the flag of the International, and Marx imagined that the masses would stay under it—what do I say?—that they would hasten along in still more formidable numbers, when he, a new Moses, had inscribed the maxims of his political decalogue on our flag in the official and binding programme of the International.

There his mistake lay. The masses, without distinction of degree of culture, religious beliefs, country and speech, had understood the language of the International when it spoke to them of their poverty, their sufferings and their slavery under the yoke of Capitalism and exploiting private ownership; they understood it when it demonstrated to them the necessity of uniting their efforts in a great solid, common struggle. But here they were being talked to about a very learned and above all very authoritarian political programme, which, in the name of their own salvation, was attempting, in that very International which was to organise their emancipation by their own efforts, to impose on them a dictatorial government, provisional, no doubt, but, meanwhile, completely arbitrary and directed by a head extraordinarily filled with brains.

Marx's programme is a complete fabric of political and economic institutions strongly centralised and very authoritarian, sanctioned, no doubt, like all despotic institutions in modern society, by universal suffrage, but subordinate nevertheless to a *very strong* government; to use the very words of Engels, the *alter ego* of Marx, the confidant of the legislator.

To what a degree of madness would not one have to be driven by ambition, or vanity, or both at once, to have been capable of conceiving the hope that one could retain the working masses of the different countries of Europe and America under the flag of the International on these conditions!

A universal State, government, dictatorship! The dream of Popes Gregory VII and Boniface VIII, of the Emperor Charles V, and of Napoleon, reproducing itself under new forms, but always with the same pretensions in the camp of Socialist Democracy! Can one imagine anything more burlesque, but also anything more revolting?

To maintain that one group of individuals, even the most intelligent and the best intentioned, are capable of becoming the thought, the soul, the guiding and unifying will of the revolutionary movement and of the economic organisation of the proletariat in all countries is such a heresy against common sense, and against the experience of history, that one asks oneself with astonishment how a man as intelligent as Marx could have conceived it.

The Popes had at least for an excuse the absolute truth which they claimed rested in their hands by the grace of the Holy Spirit and in which they were supposed to believe. Marx has not this excuse, and I shall not insult him by thinking that he believes himself to have scientifically invented something which approaches absolute truth. But from the moment that the absolute does not exist, there cannot be any infallible dogma for the International, nor consequently any official political and economic theory, and our Congresses must never claim the rôle of General Church Councils, proclaiming obligatory principles for all adherents and believers. There exists only one law which is really obligatory for all members, individuals, sections and federations in the International, of which this law constitutes the true and only basis. It is, in all its extension, in all its consequences and applications—the International solidarity of the toilers in all trades and in all countries in their economic struggle against the exploiters of labour. It is in the real organisation of this solidarity, by the spontaneous organisation of the working masses and by the absolutely free federation, powerful in proportion as it will be free, of the working masses of all languages and nations, and not in their unification by decrees and under the rod of any government whatever, that there resides the real and living unity of the International. That from this ever broader organisation of the militant solidarity of the proletariat against bourgeois exploitation there must issue, and in fact there does arise, the political struggle of the proletariat against the bourgeoisie; who can doubt? The Marxians and ourselves are unanimous on this point. But immediately there presents itself the question which separates us so profoundly from the Marxians.

We think that the necessarily revolutionary policy of the proletariat must have for its immediate and only object the destruction of States. We do not understand that anyone could speak of international solidarity when they want to keep States—unless they are dreaming of the Universal State, that is to say, universal slavery like the great Emperors and Popes—the State by its very nature being a rupture of this solidarity and consequently a permanent cause of war. Neither do we understand how anybody could speak of the freedom of the proletariat or of the real deliverance of the masses in the State and by the State. State means domination, and all domination presupposes the subjection of the masses and consequently their exploitation to the profit of some minority or other.

We do not admit, even as a revolutionary transition, either National Conventions, or Constituent Assemblies, or so-called revolutionary dictatorships; because we are convinced that the revolution is only sincere, honest and real in the masses, and that when it is concentrated in the hands of some governing individuals, it naturally and inevitably becomes reaction.

The Marxians profess quite contrary ideas. As befits good Germans, they are worshippers of the power of the State, and necessarily also the prophets of political and social discipline, the champions of order established from above downwards, always in the name of universal suffrage and the sovereignty of the masses, to whom they reserve the happiness and honour of obeying chiefs, elected masters. The Marxians admit no other emancipation than that which they expect from their so-called People's States. They are so little the enemies of patriotism that their International, even, wears too often the colours of Pan-Germanism. Between the Marxian policy and the Bismarckian policy there no doubt exists a very appreciable difference, but between the Marxians and ourselves, there is an abyss. They are Governmentalists, we are out and out Anarchists.

Indeed, between these two tendencies no conciliation to-day is possible. Only the practical experience of social revolution, of great new historic experiences, the logic of events, can bring them sooner or later to a common solution; and strongly convinced of the rightness of our principle, we hope that then the Germans themselves—the workers of Germany and not their leaders—will finish by joining us in order to demolish those prisons of peoples, that are called States and to condemn politics, which indeed is nothing but the art of dominating and fleecing the masses.

At a pinch I can conceive that despots, crowned or uncrowned, could dream of the sceptre of the world; but what can be said of a friend of the proletariat, of a revolutionary who seriously claims that he desires the emancipation of the masses and who setting himself up as director and supreme arbiter of all the revolutionary movements which can burst forth in different countries, dares to dream of the subjection of the proletariat of all these countries to a single thought, hatched in his own brain.

I consider that Marx is a very serious revolutionary, if not always a very sincere one, and that he really wants to uplift the masses and I ask myself—Why it is that he does not perceive that the establishment of a universal dictatorship, whether collective or individual, of a dictatorship which would perform in some degree the task of chief engineer of the world revolution—ruling and directing the insurrectional movement of the masses in all countries as one guides a machine—that the establishment of such a dictatorship would suffice by itself alone to kill the revolution, or paralyse and pervert all the people's movements? What is the man, what is the group of individuals, however great may be their genius, who would dare to flatter themselves to be able to embrace and comprehend the infinite multitude of interests, of tendencies and actions, so diverse in each country, province, locality, trade, and of which the immense totality, united, but not made uniform, by one grand common aspiration and by some fundamental principles which have passed henceforth into the consciousness of the masses, will constitute the future social revolution?

And what is to be thought of an International Congress which in the so-called interests of this revolution, imposes on the proletariat of the whole civilised world a government invested with dictatorial power, with the inquisitorial and dictatorial rights of suspending regional federations, of proclaiming a ban against whole nations in the name of a so-called official principle, which is nothing else than Marx's own opinion, transformed by the vote of a fake majority into an absolute truth? What is to be thought of a Congress which, doubtless to render its folly still more patent, relegates to America this dictatorial governing body, after having composed it of men probably very honest, but obscure, sufficiently ignorant, and absolutely unknown to it. Our enemies the bourgeois would then be right when they laugh at our Congresses and when they claim that the International only fights old tyrannies in order to establish new ones, and that in order worthily to replace existing absurdities, it wishes to create another!

CHAPTER V

Social Revolution
and the State

WHAT Bismarck has done for the political and bourgeois world, Marx claims to do to-day[15] for the Socialist world, among the proletariat of Europe; to replace French initiative by German initiative and domination; and as, according to him and his disciples, there is no German thought more advanced than his own, he believed the moment had come to have it triumph theoretically and practically in the International. Such was the only object of the Conference which he called together in September 1871 in London. This Marxian thought is explicitly developed in the famous Manifesto of the refugee German Communists drafted and published in 1848 by Marx and Engels. It is the theory of the emancipation of the proletariat and of the organisation of labour by the State.

Its principal point is the conquest of political power by the working class. One can understand that men as indispensable as Marx and Engels should be the partisans of a programme which, consecrating and approving political power, opens the door to all ambitions. Since there will be political power there will necessarily be subjects, got up in Republican fashion, as citizens, it is true, but who will none the less be subjects, and who as such will be forced to obey—because without obedience, there is no power possible. It will be said in answer to this that they will obey not men but laws which they will have made themselves. To that I shall reply that everybody knows how much, in the countries which are freest and most democratic, but politically governed, the people make the laws, and what their obedience to these laws signifies. Whoever is not deliberately desirous of taking fictions for realities must recognise quite well that, even in such countries, the people really obey not laws which they make themselves, but laws which are made in their name, and that to obey these laws means nothing else to them than to submit

15 i.e., 1872.

to the arbitrary will of some guarding and governing minority or, what amounts to the same thing, to be freely slaves.

There is in this programme another expression which is profoundly antipathetic to us revolutionary Anarchists who frankly want the complete emancipation of the people; the expression to which I refer is the presentation of the proletariat, the whole society of toilers, as a "class" and not as a "mass". Do you know what that means? Neither more nor less than a new aristocracy, that of the workers of the factories and towns, to the exclusion of the millions who constitute the proletariat of the countryside and who in the anticipations of the Social Democrats of Germany will, in effect, become subjects of their great so-called People's State. "Class", "Power", "State", are three inseparable terms, of which each necessary pre-supposes the two others and which all definitely are to be summed up by the words: *the political subjection and the economic exploitation of the masses.*

The Marxians think that just as in the 18th Century the bourgeoisie dethroned the nobility, to take its place and to absorb it slowly into its own body, sharing with it the domination and exploitation of the toilers in the towns as well as in the country, so the proletariat of the towns is called on to-day to dethrone the bourgeoisie, to absorb it and to share with it the domination and exploitation of the proletariat of the countryside; this last outcast of history, unless this latter later on revolts and demolishes all classes, denominations, powers, in a word, all States.

To me, however, the flower of the proletariat does not mean, as it does to the Marxians, the upper layer, the most civilised and comfortably off in the working world, that layer of semi-bourgeois workers, which is precisely the class the Marxians want to use to constitute their *fourth governing class,* and which is really capable of forming one if things are not set to rights in the interests of the great mass of the proletariat; for with its relative comfort and semi-bourgeois position, this upper layer of workers is unfortunately only too deeply penetrated with all the political and social prejudices and all the narrow aspirations and pretensions of the bourgeois. It can be truly said that this upper layer is the least socialist, the most individualist in all the proletariat.

By the *flower of the proletariat,* I mean above all, that great mass, those millions of non-civilised, disinherited, wretched and illiterates whom Messrs. Engels and Marx mean to subject to the paternal regime of *a very strong government,* to employ an expression used by Engels in a letter to our friend Cafiero. Without doubt, this will be for their own salvation, as of course all governments, as is well known, have been established solely in the interests of the masses themselves.[16] By the flower of the proletariat I mean precisely that eternal "meat" for governments, that great *rabble of the people* ordinarily designated by Messrs. Marx and Engels by the phrase at once picturesque and contemptuous of "lumpen proletariat", the "riff-raff", that rabble which, being very nearly unpolluted by all bourgeois civilisation carries in its heart, in its aspirations, in all necessities and the miseries of its collective position, all the germs of the Socialism of the future, and which alone is powerful enough to-day to inaugurate the Social Revolution and bring it to triumph.

Though differing from us in this respect also, the Marxians do not reject our programme absolutely. They only reproach us with wanting to hasten, to outstrip, the slow march of history and to ignore the scientific law of successive evolutions. Having had the thoroughly German nerve to proclaim in their works consecrated to the philosophical analysis of the past that the bloody defeat of the insurgent peasants of Germany and the triumph of the despotic States in the sixteenth century constituted a great revolutionary progress, they to-day have the nerve to satisfy themselves with establishing a new despotism to the so-called profit of the town-workers and to the detriment of the toilers in the country.

To support his programme of the conquest of political power, Marx has a very special theory which is, moreover, only a logical consequence of his whole system. The political condition of each country, says he, is always the product and the faithful expression of its economic situation; to change the former it is only necessary to transform the latter. According to Marx, all the secret of historic evolution is there. He takes no account of other elements in history, such as the quite obvious reaction of political, juridical, and religious

---

16 This sentence is, of course, purely ironical.

institutions on the economic situation. He says, "Poverty produces political slavery, the State," but he does not allow this expression to be turned around, to say "Political slavery, the State, reproduces in its turn, and maintains poverty as a condition of its own existence; so that, in order to destroy poverty, it is necessary to destroy the State!" And, a strange thing in him who forbids his opponents to lay the blame on political slavery, the State, as an active cause of poverty, he commands his friends and disciples of the Social Democratic Party in Germany to consider the conquest of power and of political liberties as the preliminary condition absolutely necessary for economic emancipation.

Yet the sociologists of the school of Marx, men like Engels and Lassalle, object against us that the State is not at all the cause of the poverty of the people, of the degradation and servitude of the masses; but that the wretched condition of the masses, as well as the despotic power of the State are, on the contrary, both the one and the other, the effects of a more general cause, the products of an inevitable phase in the economic development of society, of a phase which, from the point of view of history, constitutes true progress, an immense step towards what *they* call the social revolution. To such a degree, in fact, that Lassalle did not hesitate loudly to proclaim that the defeat of the formidable revolt of the peasants in Germany in the sixteenth century—a deplorable defeat if ever there was one, from which dates the centuries-old slavery of the Germans—and the triumph of the despotic and centralised State which was the necessary consequence of it, constituted a real triumph for this revolution; because the peasants, say the Marxians, are the natural representatives of reaction, whilst the modern military and bureaucratic State—a product and inevitable accompaniment of the social revolution, which, starting from the second half of the sixteenth century commenced the slow, but always progressive transformation of the ancient feudal and land economy into the production of wealth, or, what comes to the same thing, into the exploitation of the labour of the people by capital—this State was an essential condition of this revolution.

One can understand how Engels, driven on by the same logic, in a letter addressed to one of our friends, Carlo Cafiero, was able to say, without the least irony, but on the contrary, very seriously, that Bismarck as well as King Victor Emmanuel II had rendered immense services to the revolution, both of them having created political centralisation in their respective countries.

Likewise Marx completely ignores a most important element in the historic development of humanity, that is, the temperament and particular character of each race and each people, a temperament and character which are naturally themselves the product of a multitude of ethnographical, climatological, economic, as well as historic causes, but which, once produced, exercise, even apart from and independent of the economic conditions of each country, a considerable influence on its destinies, and even on the development of its economic forces. Among these elements and these so to say natural traits, there is one whose action is completely decisive in the particular history of each people; it is the intensity of the instinct of revolt, and by the same token, of liberty, with which it is endowed or which is has conserved. This instinct is a fact which is completely primordial and animal; one finds it in different degrees in every living being, and the energy, the vital power of each is to be measured by its intensity. In man, besides the economic needs which urge him on, this instinct becomes the most powerful agent of all human emancipations. And as it is a matter of temperament, not of intellectual and moral culture, although ordinarily it evokes one and the other, it sometimes happens that civilised peoples possess it only in a feeble degree, whether it is that it has been exhausted during their previous development, or whether the very nature of their civilisation has depraved them, or whether, finally, they were originally less endowed with it than were others.

Such has been in all its past, such is still to-day the Germany of the nobles and the bourgeoisie. The German proletariat, a victim for centuries of one and the other, can it be made jointly responsible for the spirit of conquest which manifests itself to-day in the upper classes of this nation? In actual fact, undoubtedly, no. For a conquering people is necessarily a slave people, and the slaves are always the proletariat. Conquest is therefore completely opposed to their interests and liberty. But they are jointly responsible for it in spirit, and they will remain jointly responsible as long as they do not understand that this Pan-German State, this Republican and so-called People's State, which is promised them in a more or less near future, would be nothing else, if it could ever be realised, than a new form of very hard slavery for the proletariat.

Up to the present, at least, they do not seem to have understood it, and none of their chiefs, orators, or publicists, has given himself the trouble to explain it to them. They are all trying, on the contrary, to inveigle the proletariat along a path where they will meet with nothing but the animadversion of the world and their own enslavement; and, as long as, obeying the directions of these leaders, they pursue this frightful illusion of a People's State, certainly the proletariat will not have the initiative for social revolution. This Revolution will come to it from outside, probably from the Mediterranean countries, and then yielding to the universal contagion, the German proletariat will unloose its passions and will overthrow at one stroke the dominion of its tyrants and of its so-called emancipators.

The reasoning of Marx leads to absolutely opposite results. Taking into consideration nothing but the one economic question, he says to himself that the most advanced countries and consequently the most capable of making a social revolution are those in which modern Capitalist production has reached its highest degree of development. It is they that, to the exclusion of all others, are the civilised countries, the only ones called on to initiate and direct this revolution. This revolution will consist in the expropriation, whether by peaceful succession or by violence, of the present property-owners and capitalists, and in the appropriation of all lands and all capital by the State, which in order to fulfil its great economic as well as political mission must necessarily be very powerful and very strongly centralised. The State will administer and direct the cultivation of the land by means of its salaried officers commanding armies of rural toilers, organised and disciplined for this cultivation. At the same time, on the ruin of all the existing banks it will establish a single bank, financing all labour and all national commerce.

One can understand that, at first sight, such a simple plan of organisation—at least in appearance—could seduce the imagination of workers more eager for justice and equality than for liberty and foolishly fancying that these two can exist without liberty—as if to gain and consolidate justice and equality, one could rely on other people, and on ruling groups above all, however much they may claim to be elected and controlled by the people. In reality it would be for the proletariat a barrack regime, where the standardised mass of men and women workers would wake, sleep, work and live to the beat of the drum; for the clever and the learned a privilege of governing; and for the mercenary minded, attracted by the immensity of the international speculations of the national banks, a vast field of lucrative jobbery.

At home it will be slavery, in foreign affairs a truceless war, unless all the peoples of the "inferior" races, Latin or Slav, the one tired of the bourgeois civilisation, the other almost ignorant of it and despising it by instinct, unless these peoples resign themselves to submit to the yoke of an essentially bourgeois nation and a State all the more despotic because it will call itself the People's State.

The social revolution, as the Latin and Slav toilers picture it to themselves, desire it and hope for it, is infinitely broader than that promised them by the German or Marxian programme. It is not for them a question of the emancipation parsimoniously measured out and only realisable at a very distant date, of the working class, but the complete and real emancipation of all the proletariat, not only of some countries but of all nations, civilised and uncivilised—a new civilisation, genuinely of the people, being destined to commence by this act of universal emancipation.

And the first word of this emancipation can be none other than "Liberty", not that political, bourgeois liberty, so much approved and recommended as a preliminary object of conquest by Marx and his adherents, but *the great human liberty,* which, destroying all the dogmatic, metaphysical, political and juridical fetters by which everybody to-day is loaded down, will give to everybody, collectivities as well as individuals, full autonomy in their activities and their development, delivered once and for all from all inspectors, directors and guardians.

The second word of this emancipation is *solidarity,* not the Marxian solidarity from above downwards by some government or other, either by ruse or by force, on the masses of the people; not that solidarity of all which is the negation of the liberty of each, and which by that very fact becomes a falsehood, a fiction, having slavery as the reality behind it; but that solidarity which is on the contrary the confirmation and the realisation of every liberty, having its origin not in any political law whatsover, but in the inherent collective nature of man, in virtue of which no man is free if all the men who surround him and who exercise the least influence, direct or indirect, on his life are not so equally. This truth is to be found magnificently expressed in the Declaration of the Rights of Man drafted by Robespierre, and which proclaims that *the slavery of the least of men is the slavery of all.*

The solidarity which we ask, far from being the result of any artificial or authoritarian organisation whatsoever, can only be the spontaneous product of social life, economic as well as moral; the result of the free federation of common interests, aspirations and tendencies. It has for essential bases, *equality, collective labour*— becoming obligatory for each not by the force of law, but by the force of facts—and collective property; as a directing light, experience—that is to say the practice of the collective life; *knowledge and learning;* and as a final goal the establishment of Humanity, and consequently the ruin of all States.

There is the ideal, not divine, not metaphysical but human and *practical*, which alone corresponds to the modern aspirations of the Latin and Slav peoples. They want complete liberty, complete solidarity, complete equality; in a word, they want only Humanity and they will not be satisfied, even on the score of its being provisional and transitory, with anything less than that. The Marxians will denounce their aspirations as folly; that has been done over a long period, that has not turned them from their goal, and they will never change the magnificence of that goal for the completely bourgeois platitudes of Marxian Socialism.

Their ideal is practical in this sense, that its realisation will be much less difficult than that of the Marxian idea, which, besides the poverty of its objective, presents also the grave inconvenience of being absolutely impracticable. It will not be the first time that clever men, rational and advocates of things practical and possible, will be recognised for Utopians, and that those who are called Utopians to-day will be recognised as practical men to-morrow. The absurdity of the Marxian system consists precisely in the hope that by inordinately narrowing down the Socialist programme so as to make it acceptable to the bourgeois Radicals,[17] it will transform the latter into unwitting and involuntary servants of the social revolution. There is a great error there; all the experience of history demonstrates to us that an alliance concluded between two different parties always turns to the advantage of the more reactionary of the two parties; this alliance necessarily enfeebles the more progressive party, by diminishing and distorting its programme, by destroying its moral strength, its confidence in itself, whilst a reactionary party, when it is guilty of falsehood is always and more than ever true to itself.

As for me, I do not hesitate to say that all the Marxist flirtations with the Radicalism, whether reformist or revolutionary, of the bourgeois, can have no other result than the demoralisation and disorganisation of the rising power of the proletariat, and consequently a new consolidation of the established power of the bourgeois.

---

17 Radicals—the more progressive wing of the Liberals, and standing for social reform and political equalitarianism, but not for the abolition of private property, or of the wage system. Hence they were not Socialists. The Labour Party of to-day has inherited much of their policy.

CHAPTER VI

Political Action and the Workers

IN Germany, Socialism is already beginning to be a formidable power,[18] despite restrictive and oppressive laws. The workers' parties[19] are frankly Socialist—in the sense that they want a Socialistic reform of the relations between capital and labour, and that they consider that to obtain this reform, the State must first of all be reformed, and that if it will not suffer itself to be reformed peaceably, it must be reformed by a political revolution. This political revolution, they maintain, must precede the social revolution, but I consider this as a fatal error, as such a revolution would necessarily be a bourgeois revolution and would produce only a bourgeois socialism, that is to say it would lead to a new exploitation, more cunning and hypocritical, but not less oppressive than the present.

This idea of a political revolution preceding a social revolution has opened wide the doors of the Social Democratic Party to all the Radical democrats; who are very little of Socialists. And the leaders of the Party have, against the instincts of the workers themselves, brought it into close association with the bourgeois democrats of the People's Party [the Liberals], which is quite hostile to Socialism, as its Press and politicians demonstrate. The leaders of this People's party, however, have observed that these anti-Socialist utterances displeased the workers, and they modified their tone for they need the workers' assistance in their political aims, just as it has always been the method of the bourgeoisie to carry out a revolution by means of the all-powerful arm of the people and then filch the profits for themselves. Thus these Popular democrats have now become "Socialists" of a sort. But the "Socialism" does not go beyond the harmless dreams of bourgeois co-operativism.

---

18 Written in September, 1870.
19 The Marxists and the Lassalleans. They united in 1875.

At a Congress in Eisenach, in August, 1869, there were negotiations between the representatives of the two parties, worker and democrat, and these resulted in a programme which definitely constituted the Social Democratic Labour Party. This programme is a compromise between the Socialist and revolutionary programme of the International as determined by the Congresses of Brussels and Basel, and the programme of bourgeois democracy. This new programme called for a "free People's State", wherein all class domination and all exploitation would be abolished. Political liberty was declared to be the most urgently needed condition for the economic emancipation of the working classes. Consequently the social question was inseparable from the political question. Its solution was possible only in a democratic State. The Party was declared to be associated with the International. Some immediate objectives were set out: manhood suffrage, referenda, free and compulsory education, separation of Church and State, liberty of the Press, State aid to workers' co-operatives.

This programme expresses not the Socialist and revolutionary aspirations of the workers, but the policy of the leaders. There is a direct contradiction between the programme of the International, and the purely national programme set out above, between the Socialist solidarity of Labour and the political patriotism of the National State. Thus the Social Democrats find themselves in the position of being united with their bourgeois compatriots against the workers of a foreign country; and their patriotism has vanquished their Socialism. Slaves themselves of the German Government, they fulminate against the French Government as tyrants. The only difference between Bismarck and Napoleon III was that the one was a successful and the other an unsuccessful scoundrel, one was a scoundrel, and the other a scoundrel and a half.

The German Socialists' idea of a Free State is a contradiction in terms, an unrealisable dream. Socialism implying the destruction of the State, those who support the State must renounce Socialism; must sacrifice the economic emancipation of the masses to the political power of some privileged party—and in this case it will be bourgeois democracy.

The programme of the Social Democrats really implies that they trust the bourgeois democrats to help the workers to achieve a Social revolution, after the workers have helped the bourgeois to achieve a political revolution. The way they have swallowed bourgeois ideas is shown by the list of immediate objectives, which except for the last, comprise the well-known programme of bourgeois democracy. And in fact these immediate objectives have become their real objectives, so that they have lent the Social Democratic Party to become a mere tool in the hands of the bourgeois democrats.

Does Marx himself sincerely want the antagonism of class against class, that antagonism which renders absolutely impossible any participation of the masses in the political action of the State? For this action, considered apart from the bourgeoisie, is not practicable: it is only possible when it develops in conjunction with some party of that class and lets itself be directed by the bourgeois. Marx cannot be ignorant of that, and besides, what is going on to-day in Geneva, Zurich, Basel, and all over Germany, ought to open his eyes on this point, if he had closed them, which, frankly, I do not believe. It is impossible for me to believe it after having read the speech he delivered recently at Amsterdam, in which he said that in certain countries, perhaps in Holland itself, the social question could be resolved peacefully, legally, without force, in a friendly fashion, which can mean nothing but this: it can be resolved by a series of successive, pacific, voluntary and judicious compromises, between bourgeoisie and proletariat. Mazzini never said anything different from that.[20]

Mazzini and Marx are agreed on this point of capital importance, that the great social reforms which are to emancipate the proletariat cannot be realised except in a great democratic, Republican, very powerful and strongly centralised State, which for the proper well-being of the people, in order to be able to give them education and social welfare, must impose on them, by means of their own vote, a very strong government.[21]

---

20 In a previous passage, Bakunin had said that Mazzini, like the Marxists, wanted to use the people's strength whereby to gain political power.

21 This is essentially the line put forward to-day by Labour politicians, especially when, in Australia, they are asking for increased powers for the Federal Government.

I maintain that if ever the Marxian party, that of so-called Social Democracy, continues to pursue the course of political demands, it will see itself forced to condemn, sooner or later, that of economic demands, the course of strike action, so incompatible are these two courses in reality.

It is always the same German temperament and the same logic which leads the Marxists directly and fatally into what we call Bourgeois Socialism and to the conclusion of a new political pact between the bourgeois who are Radicals, or who are forced to become such and the "intelligent", respectable, that is to say, duly bourgeoisfied minority of the town proletariat to the detriment of the mass of the proletariat, not only in the country, but in the towns also.

Such is the true meaning of workers' candidatures to the Parliaments of existing States, and that of the conquest of political power by the working class. For even from the point of view of only the town proletariat to whose exclusive profit it is desired to take possession of political power, is it not clear that the popular nature of this power will never be anything else than fiction? It will be obviously impossible for some hundreds of thousands or even some tens of thousands or indeed for only a few thousand men to effectively exercise this power. They will necessarily exercise it by proxy, that is to say, entrust it to a group of men elected by themselves to represent and govern them, which will cause them without fail to fall back again into all the falsehoods and servitudes of the representative or bourgeois regime. After a brief moment of liberty or revolutionary orgy, citizens of a new State, they will awake to find themselves slaves, playthings and victims of new power-lusters. One can understand how and why clever politicians should attach themselves with great passion to a programme which opens such a wide horizon to their ambition; but that serious workers, who bear in the hearts like a living flame the sentiment of solidarity with their companions in slavery and wretchedness the whole world over, and who desire to emancipate themselves not to the detriment of all but by the emancipation of all, to be free themselves with all and not to become tyrants in their turn; that sincere toilers could become enamoured of such a programme, that is much more difficult to understand.

But then, I have a firm confidence that in a few years the German workers themselves, recognising the fatal consequences of a theory which can only favour the ambition of their bourgeois chiefs or indeed that of some exceptional workers who seek to climb on the shoulders of their comrades in order to become dominating and exploiting bourgeois in their turn—I have confidence that the German workers will reject this theory with contempt and wrath, and that they will embrace the true programme of working-class emancipation, that of the destruction of States, with as much passion as do to-day the workers of the great Mediterranean countries, France, Spain, Italy, as well as the Dutch and Belgian workers.

Meanwhile we recognise the perfect right of the German workers to go the way that seems to them best, provided that they allow us the same liberty. We recognise even that it is very possible that by all their history, their particular nature, the state of their civilisation and their whole situation to-day, they are forced to go this way. Let then the German, American and English toilers try to win political power since they desire to do so. But let them allow the toilers of other countries to march with the same energy to the destruction of all political power. Liberty for all, and a natural respect for that liberty; such are the essential conditions of international solidarity.

The German Social Democratic Labour Party founded in 1869 by Liebknecht and Bebel, under the auspices of Marx, announced in its programme that *the conquest of political power was the preliminary condition of the economic emancipation of the proletariat,* and that consequently the immediate object of the party must be the organisation of a widespread legal agitation for the winning of universal suffrage and of all other political rights; its final aim, the establishment of the great pan-German and so-called People's State.

Between this tendency and that of the Alliance [Bakunin's organisation] which rejected all political action, not having as immediate and direct objective the triumph of the workers over Capitalism, and as a consequence, the abolition of the State, there exists the same difference, the same abyss, as between the proletariat and the bourgeoisie. The Alliance, taking the programme of the International seriously, had rejected contemptuously all compromise with bourgeois politics, in however Radical and Socialist a guise it might do itself up, advising the proletariat as the only way of real emancipation, as the only policy truly salutary for them, the exclusively *negative* policy of the demolition of political institutions, of political power, of government in general, of the State, and as a necessary consequence the international organisation of the scattered forces of the proletariat into a revolutionary power directed against all the established powers of the bourgeoisie.

The Social Democrats of Germany, quite on the contrary, advised all the workers so unfortunate as to listen to them, to adopt, as the immediate objective of their association, legal agitation for the preliminary conquest of political rights; they thus subordinate the movement for economic emancipation to the movement first of all exclusively political, and by this obvious reversal of the whole programme of the International, they have filled in at a single stroke the abyss they had opened between proletariat and bourgeoisie. They have done more than that, they have tied the proletariat in tow with the bourgeoisie. For it is evident that all this political movement so boosted by the German Socialists, since it must precede the economic revolution, can only be directed by the bourgeois, or what will be still worse, *by workers transformed into bourgeois by their ambition and vanity,* and, passing in reality over the head of the proletariat, like all its predecessors, this movement will not fail once more to condemn the proletariat to be nothing but a blind instrument inevitably sacrificed in the struggle of the different bourgeois parties between themselves for the conquest of political power, that is to say, for the power and right to dominate the masses and exploit them. To whomsoever doubts it, we should only have to show what is happenings in Germany, where the organs of Social Democracy sing hymns of joy on seeing a Congress (at Eisenach) of professors of bourgeois political economy recommending the proletariat of Germany to the high and paternal protection of States and in the parts of Switzerland where the Marxian programme prevails, at Geneva, Zürich, Basel, where the International has descended to the point of being no longer anything more than a sort of electoral box for the profit of the Radical bourgeois. These incontestable facts seem to me to be more eloquent than any words.

They are real and logical in this sense that they are a natural effect of the triumph of Marxian propaganda. And it is for that reason that we fight the Marxian theories to the death, convinced that if they could triumph throughout the International, they would certainly not fail to kill at least its spirit everywhere, as they have already done in very great part in the countries just mentioned.

The instinctive passion of the masses for economic equality is so great that if they could hope to receive it from the hands of despotism, they would indubitably and without much reflection do as they have often done before, and deliver themselves to despotism. Happily, historic experience has been of some service even with the masses. To-day, they are beginning everywhere to understand that no despotism has nor can have, either the will or the power to give them economic equality. The programme of the International is very happily explicit on this question. *The emancipation of the toilers can be the work only of the toilers themselves.*

Is it not astonishing that Marx has believed it possible to graft on this nevertheless so precise declaration, which he probably drafted himself, his *scientific Socialism*? That is to say, the organisation and the government of the new society by Socialistic scientists and professors—the worst of all despotic government!

But thanks to this great beloved "riff raff" of the common people, who will oppose themselves, urged on by an instinct invincible as well as just, to all the governmentalist fancies of this little working-class minority already properly disciplined and marshalled to become the myrmidons of a new despotism, the *scientific Socialism* of Marx will always remain as a Marxian dream. This new experience, more dismal perhaps than all past experiences, will be spared society, because the proletariat in general, and in all countries is animated to-day by a profound distrust against what is political and against all the politicians in the world, whatever their party colour, all of them having equally deceived, oppressed, exploited—the reddest Republicans just as much as the most absolutist Monarchists.

Appendix

In I. Berlin's *Karl Marx: His Life and Environment* (Home University Library) are reprinted some passages of Bakunin's writing which I have not seen elsewhere and which emphasise his views on the State, and other passages on the character of Marx. The first selection is as follows:

"We revolutionary anarchists are the enemies of all forms of State and State organisations . . . we think that all State rule, all governments being by their very nature placed outside the mass of the people, must necessarily seek to subject it to customs and purposes entirely foreign to it. We therefore declare ourselves to be foes . . . of all State organisations as such, and believe that the people can only be happy and free, when, organised from below by means of its own autonomous and completely free associations, without the supervision of any guardians, it will create its own life."

"We believe power corrupts those who wield it as much as those who are forced to obey it. Under its corrosive influence some become greedy and ambitious tyrants, exploiting society in their own interest, or in that of their class, while others are turned into abject slaves. Intellectuals, positivists,[22] doctrinaires, all those who put science before life . . . defend the idea of the state as being the only possible salvation of society—quite logically since from their false premises that thought comes before life, that only abstract theory can form the starting point of social practice . . . they draw the inevitable conclusion that since such theoretical knowledge is at present possessed by very few, these few must be put in possession of social life, not only to inspire, but to direct all popular movements, and that no sooner is the revolution over than a new social organisation must at once be set up; not a free association of popular bodies . . . working in accordance with the needs and instincts of the people, but a centralised dictatorial power, concentrated in the hands of this academic minority, as if they really expressed the popular will. . . . The difference between such revolutionary dictatorship and the modern State is only one of external trappings. In substance both are a tyranny of the minority over a majority in the name of the people—in the name of the stupidity of the many and the superior wisdom of the few; and so they are equally reactionary, devising to secure political and economic privilege to the ruling minority and the . . . enslavement of the masses, to destroy the present order only to erect their own rigid dictatorship on its ruins." (pp. 205-6)

---

[22] Followers of Auguste Comte (1798–1857) founder of the science of Sociology. In his later writings Comte advocated a Religion of Humanity, to be led by a sort of agnostic secular priesthood consisting of scientific intellectuals, who would act as the moral and spiritual guides of a new social order.

For a complete list of anarchist literature send a stamped
addressed envelope to:

Freedom Press
in Angel Alley
84b Whitechapel High Street
London E1